GIVE BACK

MARIA CAMPBELL

DOREEN JENSEN

JOY ASHAM FEDORICK

JAUNE QUICK-TO-SEE SMITH

JEANNETTE ARMSTRONG

LEE MARACLE

gallerie

Give Back:
First Nations Perspectives on Cultural Practice

Contents

Strategies for Survival

by Maria Campbell

Maria Campbell

"Strategies for Survival" was given as a talk at the Women in View festival, Vancouver, 1991.

Sometimes it seems I've spent my whole life dealing with racism. As an aboriginal woman in Canada it's part of our daily life. We get up in the morning, we check the weather, and we dress for it. As aboriginal people, we've had to do that to survive.

I didn't start writing, making films or working in theatre because of the need to create. I did that because I needed to survive.

I wrote my first book in 1969. I was working at what I call a "straight job." I was a single mother with four children to support. I was very poor with no skills. I was fired from my job and wasn't able to find anything else. I didn't have any way to feed my children. So it was a really depressing time. In 1969 I wasn't a hippy. I didn't fit in any of the places people hung out together. I was a long way from home. I needed someone to talk to and there was nobody around. I decided to write. I made the paper my friend, and talked to it. The result of that is my first book, *Halfbreed*.

What that book did was give me life. It helped me to go through a healing process, to understand where I was coming from. It helped me to stop blaming the victim, and start blaming the criminal. It helped me to realize that it wasn't my fault, that racism was real, that you could reach out and touch it, and that a lot of what happened in my life was a result of racism.

Through writing *Halfbreed*, I was able to analyze my life and my community, and to analyze the community around me. It was a very difficult process, but it gave me life. It also opened doors for me. At that point, the grandmothers gave me gifts. And those gifts became the tools for my work — work that has not only served to heal myself and my family, but also to make change in my community and the communities I live in.

When I say I don't write to create anything, I really mean

that. I wish sometimes that I had the luxury of just staying home and creating beautiful things.

Being a writer and a community worker hasn't been easy. Every day has been a struggle. I'm proud of the fact that I have raised four children by myself. I've never received a government grant — I've always been turned down by the Canada Council or whoever I applied to. I've never had a "real job" — my writing and the work from my writing has allowed me to raise four children and be able to do my work with some dignity.

I wouldn't have been able to survive without a strong community, a community of support from my peers. There haven't been a lot of people who give that kind of support, but there have been some. I always think of people walking up a hill. Some people are just about at the top of the hill. Some people are halfway up. There are some of us who get halfway and then slide all the way back down, to start again. Most of the time, people who are near the top don't bother to stop and help somebody else. But there are those people who walk up the hill with you. Sometimes they're ahead of you and sometimes they're behind you, but you know they're there when you need them. I've found that kind of support in my own community, with my own people. I've also found it in the community outside. So networking, for me, has been invaluable.

Through my writing and my work I've been able to meet other people of colour. This has widened my vision, and given me a sense of strength in solidarity.

I don't want to offend anyone — and I don't know why I say that because one of the things I've accumulated over the years is a reputation for being a "bad-assed woman." It's not easy being an aboriginal person in the arts. I feel it's easier if you are a person of color, to be a part of what's happening, to have access to things. It's been very difficult for Native writers to write their own stories, to be heard and to have their community heard. For over fifteen years we've talked about it. Now at last the issue of appropriation is being raised outside Native communities.

When I first started writing, I was treated very gently by the institutions, simply because I was the first Native writer to become well-known. *Halfbreed* was a bestseller. At the time the book was published, people seemed to want to understand what the Native community was about, and I guess the book did that.

I was very vulnerable, and very open with people. Right across the country, a lot of white people wanted to take me under their wing and help me, because they felt bad about what they read. That was all right for a little while. Those people taught me a lot. But I found that when I started to speak out, when I started to get strong, that was a whole different thing. Doors were closed to me. I wasn't able to get back into them again.

There were times also when my own people were very angry with me. By exposing myself and my own life, they felt I was perpetuating media stereotypes — that Native people were drug addicts, were on the street. It took me a long time — not to understand, but to be able to articulate for my own community — that when you are oppressed, and when you are trying to be born again, when you are trying to reclaim, you have to go through all of the pain. That's the first thing that comes out, and we have to deal with that. That's our first song.

Having doors closed to me as a writer allowed me to look more closely at myself. I had to ask, "What other kinds of skills do I have? What else can I do?" I learned that you didn't need all kinds of education and skills in order to do something. I started to study my own history and what other people wrote about it. I also started to read other peoples' history, and I tried to find a way to bring my community and other communities together. I needed to be able to see that we were sharing one earth, even if we were different colours. Perhaps I wouldn't have been able to do that work, if I had all kinds of opportunities as a writer.

I spent a long time exploring and learning to read my own language, and finding how to work with the rhythms that came from my own people. For a long time I couldn't write anything, because I didn't know how to use English. I'm articulate in English. I know it well. But when I was writing I always found that English manipulated me. Once I understood my own rhythms, the language of my people, the history of storytelling, and the responsibility of storytelling, then I was able to manipulate the language. And once I started to be able to manipulate English, I felt that was personal liberation.

I don't decide anything in my life. The grandmothers — these old ladies — always push me around, direct me, and tell me what I have to do. About five years ago they decided I should make films. I looked over my shoulder and said, "But I don't know how to make films." Yet through networking, talking to people, doing research in libraries, I began to feel "Yes, I want to do that, because that's another way to make change, another way to be able to open the door, to cut a key." Even if I don't make great films, my children will be able to make films if that's what they decide to do.

I wanted to produce films myself. My only experience in film before this was writing a script. It was a story about clear-cutting in the north and what it does to a community. A producer came along, and wanted me to change it. I made some changes, because I knew I had to compromise if I wanted to do this. Then the director came along, and he decided that the film was too gentle; it was too political.

"But Maria, we've got to have some fucking in here," the director said.

I asked him, "What does fucking have to do with clear-cutting?"

He wanted to take the relationship between the father and the daughter and change it into an incestuous relationship. He wanted a rape scene. I refused to write it.

This is where I really learned about what can happen when somebody takes the words that you write. The young woman who was cast was Native, but of all the women who auditioned, the slimmest, most beautiful girl was chosen. She couldn't act, but she was beautiful.

We went out and started shooting. I hung around, because they had put in the contract that I would be an adviser—whatever that meant, because nobody listened to me. One afternoon I was gone, and that afternoon a rape scene was made a part of that film.

The film was about a dress. You can do all kinds of things with cameras. Even if you say you are not prejudiced, when you are a camera person or the person directing, it's what you are inside that shines through. The girl was made to wear a dress without a slip underneath, and that changed the whole story. It changed the whole feeling of the show. It not only degraded her, but it made her community, her whole people, seem like they didn't care about anything.

At that time I decided, "If I ever do this again, I will have control of the whole production."

And so I started to produce films. It's very difficult to get money. Again, networking was very important, as was believing that the grandmothers would direct me to wherever I'm supposed to go. This summer I'm finishing a shoot that I've been working on for several years, a film on six traditional old women in the north. I've been doing a little bit every year. This year I've managed to raise enough money—from investors and from some old women in the community running bingo games for me—to be able to finish the shooting. The next challenge will be editing, and just today I met a woman, Ruby Truly, who has promised to help with that.

Strategies for survival.... It's really important to try and maintain a sense of humour. I've had to learn to be funny, to see the humorous side of things.

I've had to do a lot of praying. I think that prayers, regardless of where they come from, go to the same source—whether we call it Father or Mother. I choose to call it Mother.

I have faith in my community. I believe that whatever gift or power you have as an artist comes from the community, and what is most important is being able to give that back. If you don't give it back, there's not going to be anything left.

As the Gulf War rages, for the first time in many years I've been feeling very powerless. I think of all the work that all of us have done, and this war comes along and kicks the lid off racism. The war seems to allow racism to be free, and make it okay for people to stomp all over each other again. I guess it's important that we all keep working hard, and remember that we have elders in our communities.

We have elders in the arts community. I look around at the panel, and I'm the oldest one here. I feel very sad about that, because there are people who have been working for this kind of change for many many years, and it's important to make sure that those people are here.

You don't have to keep re-learning everything. We've already learned a lot of those things. Don't leave those people behind. You need them. If you're going to change anything, you can't do it without them. If you try doing it without them, you'll just repeat the same things over and over and over again, and we'll never get beyond where we are right now.

Maria Campbell

Maria Campbell was born in a Métis community located on a road allowance in Northern Saskatchewan. She left home at fifteen and came to Vancouver, but in her twenties she went back to the prairies where she became a community worker, activist and organizer. In the late 1960's, feeling that there was "a desperate need to do more than organize," she turned to writing. Her autobiography, *Halfbreed* (Toronto: McClelland and Stewart, 1973), became a bestseller.

In the introduction to that book, Campbell writes, "Going home after so long a time, I thought that I might find again the happiness and beauty I had known as a child. But as I walked down the rough dirt road, poked through the broken old buildings and thought back over the years, I realized that I could never find that here. Like me the land had changed, my people were gone [*ed:* the community was evicted], and if I was to know peace I would have to search within myself. That is when I decided to write about my life....I write this for all of you, to tell you what it is like to be a Halfbreed woman in our country. I want to tell you about the joys and sorrows, the oppressing poverty, the frustrations and the dreams."

Campbell has continued to write in many forms including drama, filmscripts, children's books, radio plays, magazine articles and fiction. The film of which she speaks in this article, *The Red Dress* (1977), is distributed through the National Film Board. A recent book, *The Book of Jessica: A Theatrical Transformation,* (Toronto: The Coach House Press, 1989), is an extraordinary account of a difficult collaboration between Campbell and Linda Griffiths writing the award-winning play *Jessica.*

In addition to writing, Campbell continues to work as an activist, community organizer and spokesperson for the rights of Métis people. She is also a widely respected educator. She organized workshops for Native writers in the 1980's, taught at the West Coast Women in Words summer writing retreat in 1991, and in 1992 she began teaching creative writing at the University of Saskatchewan in Saskatoon.

For the past several years, Campbell has concentrated on writing, directing and producing her own films which document the lives and ideas of Native elders.

Art History
by Doreen Jensen

Doreen Jensen, *Nax'nok Mask,* carved birch with incised designed painted black, red and blue-green; moveable eyes; horsehair hair and baleen eyelashes (from a whale's mouth), 9" × 7½"

Doreen Jensen, photo: Alexis MacDonald Seto

"Art history" was given as a talk at the Museum of Civilization, Hull, Quebec, 1992, for the opening of "Indigena: Perspectives of Indigenous Peoples on Five Hundred Years."

In my language, there is no word for "Art." This is not because we are devoid of Art, but because Art is so powerfully integrated with all aspects of life, we are replete with it. For the sake of brevity and clarity, I will use the word "Art" tonight.

This exhibition and forum, "Indigena," asks us to reflect on the impact of European colonization on indigenous cultures. In my talk, I'd like to offer a different perspective. I would like to remind you of the Art that the Europeans found when they arrived in our country.

The Europeans found Art everywhere. In hundreds of flourishing, vital cultures, Art was fully integrated with daily life. They saw dwellings painted with abstract Art that was to inspire generations of European painters. Ceremonial robes were intricately woven Art that heralded the wearers' identity and privilege in the community. Utilitarian objects, including food vessels, storage containers, and clothing, were powerfully formed and decorated with the finest, most significant Art.

Each nation had its theatre, music, and choreography. The first Europeans found hundreds of languages in use — not dialects but languages. And in every language, our Artists created philosophical argument and sacred ceremony, political discourse, fiction, and poetry.

The Europeans saw Earth Art and large-scale environmental Art projects. From the East to the West Coast, what were later called petrogylphs and pictographs recorded our histories. My own earliest memories of Art are of the tall sculptures that told the long histories of my people. These tall sculptures are called "totem poles," like the ones you see here in the Great Hall of the Museum of Civilization.

When the Europeans arrived, they found aboriginal Artists creating beauty, culture, and historical memory. Art built bridges between human life and the natural world. Art mediated between material and spiritual concerns. Art stimulated our individuality, making us alert and alive. It affirmed our cultural identities.

I say all this to honour our cultural accomplishments. As Aboriginal Artists, we need to reclaim our own identities, through our work, our heritage and our future. We don't need any longer to live within others' definitions of who and what we are. We need to put aside titles that have been imposed on our creativity — titles that serve the needs of other people. For too long our Art has been situated in the realm of anthropology by a discourse that validates only white Artists.

Today there are many Art forms of the First Nations which are still not being recognized. Think of the exquisite sea grass baskets from the West Coast of Vancouver Island, the quill work and moose hair tufting Arts of the people east of the Rockies, and ceremonial robes, woven and appliqued, throughout North America. Not surprisingly, these exquisite works of Art are mainly done by women.

Art can be a universal language which helps us bridge the gaps between our different cultures. But attitudes towards Art reveal racism. The first Europeans called our Art "primitive" and "vulgar." Today, people of European origin call our Art "craft" and "artifact."

Our elders have nurtured the important cultural traditions against tremendous odds. It is time for us to sit still, and let these powerful, precious teachings come to us. Our elders bequeathed us a great legacy of communication through the Arts.

Art is essential, for all of us. Artists are our spiritual advisers. In another five hundred years, who is going to remember Prime-Minister-What's-His-Name or Millionaire-What's-His-Name? Our cultural life — our art — is all we will be remembered by.

I believe that culture is the soul of the nation. Canada *is* the First Nations. Canada *is* the English and the French who have struggled to make a new world here. Canada *is* also the other cultures who come to make a new life. The culture of the Indigenous people is the fertile soil where these new cultures are flourishing.

Think of the important Iroquois symbol of the eagle with five feathers in its talons. Because it is such a powerful image, the American government appropriated it to use as its insignia and cultural identity. This is just one tiny example of the unacknowledged appropriation of Indian Art which has nourished North American culture for five centuries.

As we enter this new age that is being called "The Age of Information," I like to think it is the age when healing will take place. This is a good time to acknowledge our accomplishments. This is a good time to share. We need to learn from the wisdom of our ancestors. We need to recognize the hard work of our predecessors which has brought us to where we are today. We need to look to the future, and to where we can incorporate our own wisdom and vision in a healing culture for all peoples.

During the Oka crisis, Canada's mask slipped to reveal the ugly and treacherous face of racism. At last, people could see the many injustices that need to be changed in order for Canada to become a strong country. Some cultural institutions have opened their doors a crack, and begun to take initiatives to mend the cultural fabric of Canada. All cultural institutions need to begin dialogues with Aboriginal people, and develop frameworks within which we can work together on a just representation of Aboriginal cultures.

First Nations Artists have something vitally important to offer — a new (or ancient) aesthetic, a way of understanding Art and the world that can heal this country, and help us all to find a place in it.

For North West Coast Indian Artists, the act of creativity comes from the cosmos. That is what I have been told by the old people. When I'm making Art, I am one with the universe. You can see it in the work, if you look with your heart, as well as your mind. If you really pay attention, you can "get the message" — and make it your own, without diminishing it or appropriating it.

If we pay attention, First Nations Art will remind us of this basic rule for being a human being: When I diminish others' "belongingness" in the universe, my own "belongingness" becomes uncertain.

Canada is an image which hasn't emerged yet. Because this country hasn't recognized its First Nations, its whole foundation is shaky. If Canada is to emerge as a nation with cultural identity and purpose, we have to accept First Nations Art, and what it has to tell us about the spirit and the land.

Our Art is our cultural identity; it's our politics. The late George Manuel said, "This land is our culture." I add to that, "Our culture is this land." Whether you acknowledge it or ignore it, the land and the culture are one. Land claims have to be settled, before Canadians can look at themselves in the mirror and see an image they would be proud to see.

George Erasmus said, "What has happened in the last five-hundred years is not important. What is important is what we do in the next five-hundred years."

Everywhere it is a time for choices. There is still white water ahead. The choices we make today can alter our course forever, not only nationally but throughout the world.

Today is a time to share, a time to enjoy the glory of your achievements. I congratulate all of you who have made this exhibition possible: the curators, the writers, and the museum. Most importantly, I thank you, the artists — who have shared your personal visions.

Doreen Jensen, *Old Lady with Lip Labret,* (sign of a noble woman), inlaid with abalone shell, human hair, eagle feathers, stained aquamarine blue. "The blue colour really gave her a supernatural look," Jensen comments. "She's powerfully weird looking."

21

Dialogue between two masks by Doreen Jensen

left: Doreen Jensen with her mother, Clara Harris, at the book launch for *Robes of Power,* 1987, showing contemporary and traditional clothes designed and made by Doreen Jensen. Jensen has been designing clothing since 1968.

Doreen Jensen, *Grizzly-Bear Headdress,* work in progress

Doreen Jensen

Doreen Jensen's original name is Hahl Yee, a name belonging to the Killer Whale family crest from the House of Geel, of the Fireweed Clan. Her first language is Gitksan, and her parents trained her in the arts, ideas and histories of the Gitksan. "I was also expected to appreciate the value of learning English," Jensen comments. "My dad told me, 'Learn the tools of the white man — but don't forget who you are.' "

Jensen's English schooling began in a one-room schoolhouse in Kispiox, her home community. She continued at Alberni Residential School and a newly integrated public high school in Prince Rupert.

From her earliest years, she was a talented artist, winning an award at age eleven. She is a graduate of the Kitanmax school of North West Coast Indian Art.

Jensen describes herself as a "traditional Gitksan artist," noting that the designation encompasses her work as a teacher, historian, community organizer, mother, grandmother and political activist as well as a visual artist. Her contemporary art practice includes performance art, sculpture, dance, songs, writing and fabric art.

Jensen is a founding member of many organizations, including 'Ksan Association and the Society of Canadian Artists of Native Ancestry. She was instrumental in organizing the Third National Native Indian Artists Symposium in Hazelton in 1983. She works actively to promote recognition of Native women artists, and she organized an Aboriginal Women Artists' Retreat in 1987.

She is a central resource for the University of British Columbia Museum of Anthropology, where she curated the renowned exhibition *Robes of Power*, and wrote a book by the same name published in 1986. She is on the Board of Trustees of the Museum of Nature in Ottawa. As part of a collective called "The Book Builders," she wrote and researched materials for the Kitanmax School of Northwest Coast Indian Art. She was invited by *B.C. Studies* journal to guest edit a special issue, *In Celebration of Our Survival: The First Nations of British Columbia*, published in 1991, and reissued as a trade book by University of B.C. Press.

For most of her adult life, Jensen has worked tirelessly to promote aboriginal cultures, to give Native peoples place and voice, and to claim some space in Canada's major art museums for contemporary Native art.

Her work has won her many honors, including the highest award of the Professional Native Women's Association, the Golden Eagle Feather, and the honorary name of Eik'awiga (meaning Precious Jewel), which was bestowed on her in 1987 at the last potlach given by Chief James Auld Sewid and his family. This summer she was awarded an Honorary Doctorate of Letters by the University of British Columbia.

Fencepost Sitting and How I Fell Off to One Side

by Joy Asham Fedorick

Joy Asham Fedorick, photo: Kil-Young Yoo

Albert Einstein was being interviewed by a reporter about a recent scientific discovery. At the end of the interview, the reporter asked Einstein for his home phone number to check out the technical facts pre-publication to ensure their accuracy.

Einstein went over to the phone book, looked under the E's and told the reporter his telephone number. Shocked, the reporter said: "But, you're Albert Einstein and you have to look in the phone book because you can't remember your own telephone number!!!"

Einstein sighed his reply: "I use my brain to think."

It wouldn't be fair of me to expect you to read this, without letting you know what you are in for. It's a participatory article, requiring some work from you. Gosh, don't put it down, you might enjoy it.

Parts of this writing will require you to transfer information: the use of analogy is strongly relied upon. Some basic and familiar literary structures have been ignored, as have other barriers that prevent conceptual and cultural understandings to occur. In this way, this writer has attempted to replicate, in English, some of the texture of Aboriginal experience.

Think of this as a paint-by-number reading experience: analogies, footnotes, boxes full of examples, quotes, anecdotes are used to reinforce themes and scatter your linear, herded thought patterns into a right-brain intuitive mode. Not scientific you say!! Bah, Humbug!! If one believes the issue of who tells our stories can be addressed through scientific theory, statistical analysis of dependent and independent variables with cost-benefit ratios applied, put this article down right now. I talk of texture, etiquette, truth, thought, philosophy, caring, altruism, commitment. These commodities are somewhat immeasurable, and, within present society, scarce.

Reading hint: it may help to read the italicized passages and the footnotes first — you may avoid flipping!

Telling Our Stories — Who should do it?

Okay, now that I've set the stage for three-D reading, it might help you to know why I am writing this article. Seems that there has been a bit of controversy concerning ownership of stories and concepts Native.

I was asked for my opinion on these matters, Native writer that I am, and felt the answer on many levels: *knee-jerk,* That's Ours!!, survival, Our Culture is Dying!!, *sympathetic,* Who am I to say who can and cannot write whatever?, *matronizing,* Some of my best friends are non-Native writers, artists and educators ... *querying,* Why would others want to write about us? *critical,* Do they use our stories and concepts as well as we do?

I realized that maybe these are questions that others have and maybe I could form the words with curled fingertips on keyboard and answer them with thought ...

Querying: Why would others want to write about us?

I believe there are several reasons for this phenomenon. We're interesting. We seem to strike a chord with both the bigot and the revolutionary: one for the purpose of oppression and suppression, the other for the purpose of cause. We seem to have influenced even the Pope to look at our spirituality. Environmentalists are beginning to look and say, how could this continent survive for thousands of years before we came ... maybe the First Ones here knew and know something.

Yes, we're interesting to look at, analyze and speculate upon, take under advisement and pray for. All these things also fulfill a further purpose: during the scrutiny of us, one procrastinates from looking at "self."

This statement may seem harsh, and, by no means do I mean to blanket everyone with tar. I believe the Pope is well-intended and that there are others of altruistic motivation. There are also other motivations, such as theses subjects, the growing market for things-remotely-Native, and the need to exercise power.

THE SOCIOLOGIST

I was at a feminist dinner one night, when, sitting across from me was a Caucasian female sociologist. She was practicing Cocktail Anthropology (Footnote 1) on me and badgering me with endless questions about "what is it really like to be a Native woman." I was hungry and wanted to eat.

Sometimes we evade these questions, you know, just wanting to be. But finally, figuring if I ever was going to eat in peace, I'd better answer. I told her what it's like in this skin, the good, the bad, the perceived ugly, and, once more, picked up my fork.

"That's not what it's like at all," she said.

At times, envy enters it—who wouldn't want to paint like a Norval Morriseau or Rebecca Belmore? Imitation is considered the highest form of flattery—but is it good art?

Critical: Do they use our stories and concepts as well as we do?

World renowned British philosopher and sage, C. S. Lewis, in Mere Christianity, *talks of a beam of sunlight coming through a hole in a barn roof. There are three ways of perceiving that beam: you can look at it and see just the surface of the beam; you can look along it and see the edge of the beam and the sun and the sky through the hole in the roof; or, you can be within it and feel the warmth and texture of its caress, and actually **know** the beam.*

In 1986, I coordinated the Third Nishnawbe-Aski Writers' Conference in Sudbury. Saul Williams (Footnote 2), well-known visual artist from Weagemow, Ontario, attended and shared his incredible ability to capture visual wisdoms in both illustrations and words. He wrote of the first time he came out of Weagemow: "I was fourteen and fifteen ... when I saw my first TV. It looked like a suitcase with a window to nothing ..."

Our cultural perceptions and first-hand experience within the beam, allow us to communicate cultural texture. Plain words, basic language, grammatical structures that do not impair our expressiveness are used freely, directly and spiritually.

I have coined the term "literary hierarchy" to refer to the literary structure known as "beginning, middle and end." The parallel in Western theology is Creation through Apocalypse. But, if you believe in a Continuum, concepts are formed in an entirely different manner.

Our legends tell of Tricksters and Giants and mirror the follies of man. Continuous reflection on the nature of Human Beings. Our "taboo-systems" are characterized in the scrapes, scuffles, scabs and scatology of Little Shadows (Footnote 3) and Mega-Imps.

Our stories reflect long-term planning. They do not

necessarily have a beginning, middle and end. We are told that when it is essential for us to understand the wisdom of the recounting, that piece of knowledge will be there. And it is.

Our stories reflect life as it really is, and are not "formula" oriented. There is no beginning, there is an always was, and with no end there is an always will be ... The spiritual nature of the concept of the Continuum is addressed through style and with language that is relationship-oriented rather than thing-oriented. English, with its noun predominance does not allow, within rigid hierarchical style criterion, for relationships to be explored, relationships that help us to understand our place and value in the Big Picture. Native writers, tend, as Native people do, to use verbs and adjectives freely. This textured way with English provides concept and depth and warmth and fuzzy wuzzies. Helps us feel good, and just plain feel. And out of the subliminal influence of this style the spiritual circle is strengthened.

I have talked here of the way many of us are. How we verbally express ourselves. But, intrinsic to the communication of cultural concept in whatever artistic medium, is knowledge of the subject. More is known of the beam from within the beam than by looking at it.

There is another way to perceive the beam, though, that I have not alluded to as yet.

DOUBLE WAMPUM

When the Mohawk Nations first exchanged commitments of cultural respect with representatives of the British Monarchy, they honoured the British with gifts of double wampum belts. The belts, in the wampum beadwork, always included two parallel lines of coloured work. These parallel lines represented two canoes gliding along the same waters, not interfering with

*each other, yet going in the same direction.
Such was meant to represent the two
cultures: sharing equally of the Creator's
gifts, but not imposing on one another.*

There are those who can look along our beam, travel in the
same direction and not impose. At times their presence in
the same waters is soothing and helpful ... and, they not
only truly want to help but are the only ones who can ...

ROBERT BRINGHURST

*For a while I worked as an editor in the
field of Aboriginal book production. We
were attempting to establish a Native
language publishing house, with our own
imprint. We found out many things: block
funding from Canada Council would only be
available to us once we had published a
minimum of four titles, for at least two
consecutive years.*

*There was a catch, though, making this
hurdle even more difficult. The catch was,
that, due to the fact that we wanted to
publish in Ojibway and/or Cree, none of our
books could be counted towards the four
annually required. This was due to the fact
that Ojibway and Cree were not considered
Official Languages. We were told, "make
the books half English translation and we
may consider them."*

*Now, our purpose for wanting Aboriginal
language publications was not commercial
in nature: our languages are dying through
lack of support systems, and, if you know
Those-Who-Walk-With-Two-Legs in the same
way I do, you know that we like to take the*

course of least resistance. In other words, because we are surrounded by English, and adequate supplies of writings in our own languages do not exist, we have come to a place of ease with English that we may not have with our own written languages. A half and half publication would be defeating our purpose. One would have to be very dedicated indeed, to not flip to the back and take the easy-English way out.

I thought and thought. Canada Council would not listen to us, nor were they ready to make exception. Ahah!! We will make the other half French, I thought, and we would fulfill two purposes: no flipping to English, due to ease, but, should the books be used in schools, they could be dually beneficial, providing support materials for French classes as well. Now, on the surface this appeared a good temporary solution. But, I have the unfortunate ownership of something called "conscience." I realized that the budget at Canada Council for Francophone publications was severely limited. If it was manipulated by us to also support Aboriginal language publications, it would detract from Francophone cultural expression. A moral dilemma.

There are knights in shining armour, you know. Robert Bringhurst (Footnote 4), non-Native Canadian poet extraordinaire, galloped to the rescue. Highly thought of by Canada Council, he made our case for us. This time, they listened and the policy was changed.

Knights in shining armour are not confined to the Middle Ages, nor are some policies of cultural control as exercised in

Canada. Robert's advocacy and subsequent policy change by Canada Council took place in 1987.

Matronizing: Some of my best friends are non-Native writers, artists and educators ...

ADELE KOZY

I had the fantastic opportunity of being part of the Baffin Writers' Project in January/ February 1990. My role was to provide to Pond Inlet community and school creative writing workshops. I worked closely with students and teachers and focussed my day-work in the school. At night I undertook community doings and otherwise enjoyed billeting with an Inuit family.

I soon came to realize that, in the very dark months of constant nighttime North of the Arctic Circle, that internal timeclocks change, at least, seemed to, in relationship to mine. Home and family visiting, friendly conversations and amiable silences lasted till two or three in the morning. I enjoyed this, although at times, an early rise next day was difficult.

I seemed to be not the only one with 9-o'clock-sharp problems. The school seemed to have a somewhat disused air in the mornings, and, gradually, as the day progressed, the rustle and rumble of students increased. At four, one day, I entered a senior classroom to discuss the "play-in-progress" with the class teacher, Adele Kozy (Footnote 5). I expected to find her student-free and available.

Instead, a glowing and energetic group of

*senior students with that anxious-to-learn
look on their faces were grouped around
Adele. Disentangling herself from the rabid
young scholars, she came over to me. I
explained that I was sorry to interrupt her,
that I didn't know she had a class. Adele
answered:*

*"Now is the time of day they are willing
and ready to learn. A great opportunity.
Let's use it."*

*One teacher changed so the many
students didn't have to.*

There is a difference between education and learning, just as
there is between intelligence and wisdom. Wise Adele.

Sympathetic: Who am I to say who can and cannot write whatever?

In sorting this out, I had to ruminate a bit on the censorship
issue. A bannock and tea, apple-pie and Motherhood, don't
touch with a ten-foot fencepost (Footnote 6) issue. The kind
of issue that has allowed anti-Semitism (Footnote 7)
education to take place in Canada, the kind of altruistic goal
conveniently used by the "other side." Now, I say other
side, because there really are Positive and Negative forces. I
do not believe that I can move into consensus with everyone
around me, lest my own integrity be lost. I can examine my
own ethics, and, sometimes, smack dab, there I am:
opposed, not consensed and, certainly not willing to move
into the middle and be a part of the problem. Some
compromises are not good for the soul.

So, if I were to tell the producers of Native-image art and
artwords (Footnote 8) that I wanted to censor them, they
would likely knee-jerk. (Is there an echo in this room?)
Instead, all I can do is suggest and hope that the well-

intended may want to carry their intentions through to result and do so courteously, by respecting both us and our wishes.

WINDOWS OF THE SOUL

Dominant culture of North America dictates the use and reliance on eye contact as a means of determining sincerity, honesty, self-confidence, etc. Yet, to the Swampy Cree, etiquette required that you avoid direct eye contact as much as possible, as the eyes were considered to be the Windows of the Soul.

For one to stare into your eyes was an intrusion, and to focus on another's was earnestly avoided. Negative stereotypes were not assigned to this behaviour, indeed, the person who practiced such avoidance was considered to be both respectful and humble.

What I suggest to the non-Native arts producer then, is that you examine your own filter-screen, pick out the lint, and, if altruism is found in what's left, communicate your message. You may still get roasted, but, at least you have fulfilled your fundamental responsibilities of your own etiquette, and maybe learned some of ours. Regardless, you have learned to use the right fork.

Sometimes, progress requires more than etiquette — that is, the reaching out and welcoming of others — it requires competition to be set aside and cooperation to be put in its stead. This is the very real and significant role that non-Native artists and consumers of art can play, helping us to bring down the barriers that stand in our way to full creative and cultural expression.

My father (Footnote 9) and I were watching television one night and the story we viewed was set on a sheep ranch. Being a watcher of Other Human Beings, I was particularly interested in how smart the dogs were: they herded, they looked for the lost and wandering lambs, they protected from and warned of danger.

I said to Dad: "I don't know how they can be trained like that. I wish I knew the secret. Their trainers must be very clever."

Dad answered: "The secret is simple, they are not trained by man. They are trained by the other dogs."

You can help teach an old sheep-dog new tricks ... help us train and sensitize others ...

My rambling thought patterns did not stop there: I went on to look at my own life-learning and found that, gosh, I don't learn best by being "outlawed." I no longer spend days horn-locked in splay-footed discussions and verbal coercions. I now spend time with the willing, and share my own willingness to learn with them. Only the unwilling need to be policed (Footnote 10). For the willing, maybe some self-censorship would work ... the following is a self-inventory check-list for the well-intended non-Native artist contemplating the use of concepts and stories native.

SELF-CENSORSHIP CHECKLIST

The Ethical and Protocol Positives:

☐ *Am I doing this with permission, both before undertaking and before releasing completed artwork or writing?*

☐ *Do I have consent of those affected?*

☐ *Have I attempted to use "as near as ... that man's words" (Footnote 11)?*

☐ *Have I "given their dues to the folk I have described" (Footnote 12)?*

☐ *Am I being humble? honest? responsible? caring? open-minded and aware of my own filter screens?*

☐ *Am I doing this to support the emergence of Aboriginal artists?*

☐ *Am I art-driven?*

☐ *Am I courteous and fair?*

The Disgruntling Negatives:

☐ *Am I caricaturizing instead of characterizing and thus increasing negative stereo-types?*

☐ *Am I commercially-driven?*

☐ *Am I reading my own cultural interpretation into what I perceive?*

☐ *Am I failing to credit sources?*

☐ *Are my intentions destructive?*

☐ *Am I being arrogant? dishonest? untruthful? disrespectful?*

Needless to say, I hope those contemplating using our stories and concepts check off everything in the first section, and none in the second. If this is not so, there is always hope that one day Jimminy Cricket (Footnote 13) will visit ...

Knee-jerk: That's Ours!!
Survival: Our Culture is Dying!!

Last year, while in attendance at a national meeting of an alternative arts group, I took part in a debate on the question of ownership of things and concepts Native. What surprised me was a rather hostile remark by the "other side" when a Native colleague used a quote from a non-Native source. The hostile remark was a fine piece of rationalization: if Native people did not want their stories and concepts used, why, he asked, was my colleague quoting a non-Native?

There are several reasons for this, some very obvious. We, due to the dominance of Western European culture in our lives, have had our own history torn from us and thrown away. We are forced to live without our history, due to the intervention of invasion. And, in this case, my colleague was being challenged for using a cross-cultural example. Once again, the "blaming the victim" cycle in action. However, we maintain the place of etiquette, credit the speaker/originator/writer, knowing full well that this is mere courtesy, like using the right fork. We know the rules. What constantly faces us, though, is the rule-makers use a spoon.

A more subtle reason addresses the issue I call "over-specialization." Dominant society has narrowed the focus of life to be strictly material achievement (ie, dollars and jobs) and has funneled students, Native and non-Native alike, into dizzying heights of technical and professional expertise that has excluded the more generalist and spiritually-oriented, holistic, analogous thinking process one can achieve from not just one teacher or area of specialty, but from many. The kind of thinking required from you in this article.

We do not, as others discount our ability to project learning, discount this ability in others. We know that life has many teachers and that all wisdom is neither concentrated in one Human Being, nor in one area of specialty. I don't confine myself to olde English literature, nor do I voraciously devour only computer magazines. Much of my learning is from listening, participating in and feeling life. These things then become my history, my tools for the future.

One may say the same, perhaps, of non-Natives using things and concepts Native. But, a much larger reared-ugly-head emerges: it is not dominant culture and language that are in fear of demise. Don't force us over the buffalo jump to cultural extinction, either through watering down our cultural integrity or making us survive culturally anemic. When you have let us write our own hundreds and thousands of books, filled concert halls, galleries, stages with our cultural expression, then, and only then, when our culture surrounds us, living, breathing, acting, developing, secure: tell us then not to use your words, look at your art, use your tools to paint and play. How jealous the heckler of my colleague seems, to begrudge her use of a non-Native example, especially when the originator was fully credited.

And, here, I finally get off the fencepost and hold hands with Mother Earth and say: for those of you who want to know what Aboriginal people are like, let us tell you. Participate in our writings, feel our visual art, move with our music, hear in your heart our stories. For those of you who would rather do art about us, then get to know us. Then comes the next and major step: get to know yourself. Re-examine your motives. If they equal Robert Bringhurst's and Adele Kozy's — go for it. I know there are those out there that do art for the same reason I write: I can't help it.

For others, a few words from Chaucer — *The Canterbury Tales*. I dedicate these to W.P. Kinsella:

"Whoever tells a man's tale should use as near as he can that man's own words, however rude (Footnote 14) they may be; or else, by finding other words, he might tell

the tale untruly. Forgive me, too, if I have not given their dues to the folk I have described; my wits are poor, as you must be aware."

A word about Einstein: he explored philosophy, theology and art and credited these as the sources of his creative, scientific thought. A scientist or professional cannot be great unless she opens her mind to the generalist experience. I find the root of creativity exists in the reassembly of basic information, but in a new and original way. And then, once in a while the imagination floods with the awareness of the eagle, and there's this thing called Inspiration. Inspiration is definitely from a source that cannot be seen, heard, touched, tasted, sniffed or folded, stapled, mutilated. Yet, it cannot be denied. It makes beadwork out of keyboard, calico of handi-wrap and moosehide of vinyl. Inspiration, imagination: not high-tech tools, but grounded, culturally-based, and, oh-so-definitely in the beam.

This article could have been written in technical nomenclature and points made through the comparison of dearth of Native-written literature to the excess of non-Natives writing about us. It could have led you by the hand, or been a lecture. In doing so, it would have ignored the best Nation: no, not Canada, Mr. Mulroney, but, the Imagi-Nation (Footnote 15).

Have I required you to work? to think? or, is just some small haze of confusion lurking behind the Windows of your Soul? Any of these doings are worth the writing of this, even the latter. We are told that confusion always precedes periods of understanding ...

— **Joy Asham Fedorick** (Footnote 16)

Footnotes

1. Cocktail Anthropology. Poem by Aboriginal poetess Skyros Bruce, Tawow, circa 1972. Complete poem:

Cocktail Anthropology
Want to measure how long
My fingernails grow

Skyros: please call, write, I want more words from you!!!

2. Saul Williams. Little Crane Clan of Weagemow, Ontario. Visual Artist, Photographer, Teacher, Writer. Illustrated completely in one day at the Conference, the Chaka-Pesh and the Moon Legend. Then, he put down his art-tools and we found out that he could write, man, really write. Then, he finished off his week by giving art instructions to Lil Beavers. He told us at the end: "I didn't know I could be useful." Gosh, Humility in incredible action.

3. Little Shadows: Chaka-Pesh, for example, legendary boy, mischievous and unable to listen to direction, even knowing the consequences. Indian legends and stories are peopled with such characters, reflecting the very nature of man him/herself.

4. Robert Bringhurst: Author of *Pieces of Map, Pieces of Music* and all sorts of other neat stuff. Resource person to the Second and Third Nishnawbe-Aski Writers' Conferences, 1986 & '87. Supporter and promoter of Native artistic and cultural self-determination.

5. Adele Kozy: Teacher of senior students at Pond Inlet School, N.W.T. Understands and transmits that the primary purpose of her work is for the students to learn, not fit into rigidly imposed and culturally incompatible boxes. Thanks Adele.

6. fencepost: Play on words: Frank Fencepost, one of W.

P. Kinsella's major characters in books written about life through the eyes of Indian people.

7. It is a little-known fact, but **Hitler was an artist.** He painted very realistic, military structures on canvas. His work varied from copying buildings that already existed, to putting on canvas the buildings he wanted constructed. There is no guarantee that just because a person is an artist, that they are honourable and good.

8. artwords: word coined by author, quite accidentally. Others might call it a typo. I don't ignore such slips, because sometimes they say things a writer can understand: the product of creating art with words. As a lay-linguist I also am well aware that coining is a major way of keeping language alive.

9. Father: Orton M. Asham. Cree Nation, Native Veteran, wise young man.

10. Ursula Franklin. Environmentalist. Vision TV, videotape key-note address, Women and Environments Conference, Toronto, 1990.

11. Tales from Chaucer—The Canterbury Tales, done into prose by Eleanor Farjeon. p. 14. Published by The Medici Society Ltd. Reissued, Crown 8vo, 1948, printed in Great Britain at the Chiswick Press, London, N.II.

12. Ibid.

13. Jimminy Cricket. Walt Disney character from the movie Pinnochio. Jimminy would sit on Pinnochio's shoulder and whisper in his ear what the right thing was to do.

14. rude: not as familiarly used these days, the Webster Dictionary presents a definition that seems to carry the intent of Chaucer "roughly put together."

15. Imagi-nation: stolen from Santa Claus quote in the movie Miracle on Thirty-Fourth Street. Circa 1945.

16. Joy Asham Fedorick is a cultural activist who is of the Cree Nation. She spends all her time, with the exception of errands, writing and/or talking about it. Other diversions include chasing cats off the keyboard of her computer, where desk-top publishing is also undertaken. Involved for centuries in community development, spiritual matters occupy her these days, and the moving forward, through accurate, factual and ethics-based information, the quality of life in the Native community. Circa 1947.

Floating Footnote to be applied everywhere: There are no absolutes, including this one.

Originally Printed in *Artscraft Magazine,* 1991

Decolonizing Language:
Reflections on Style

by Joy Asham Fedorick

Little Spirit Tree, photo: Joy Asham Fedorick

"Fencepost Sitting and How I Fell Off to One Side," an essay I wrote in the summer of 1990 about appropriation by non-Aboriginal people of our stories, concepts and art, was for me a statement of revolution. For the first time, I wrote without hierarchical sentence structures, story formulae, formal jargon and third-person tenses. Instead, I used a storytelling style, one that requires analogous thinking. The story of how I came to this style begins when I was very young ...

Grade 4

I was a lonesome child, given to daydreaming and isolation. I wasn't raised in my home community, but in many communities the world over — my father was one of the many Aboriginal people who found that staying in the army post-war was a way to eat and a means to ensure that his country would not get lost again. The many schools and diverse communities meant two things to my girlhood: loss of Aboriginal roots and the inability for friendship bonding. My world became my dreams and my ideas and the colour that vividly surrounded me in the changing environments of my youth.

I dabbled in painting but never had the training and/or talent required to do more than that. And I had ideas trapped within me, rattling around and demanding freedom. I somehow knew that if I was a visual artist, I might be able to express these concepts, might be able to finally speak ideas and free them. But I could not paint.

I stumbled upon writing as a means to release some of this energy, and being a writer became a large part of my dreams. But I was trapped — trapped in English, in English structures, with English ideas of story content and formula, with English ideas of values.

Single Parenthood — the return to roots

In 1974, baby on either hip, I finally returned to my roots. I began working in the core area of Winnipeg — working at community development with women and streetkids. I had been raised by my English mother to tell people how lovely they looked in their new dress, even if it was a lie, how to cross my ankles, not my legs. Appearances were all important.

And, there I was, in Canada's hotspot, working with my own people ... people who told me what they really thought, about the world, about life, about me ...

I discovered .... TRUTH .... the honesty, the ability to actually see things that were basically wrong, talk about them, not layer bandaids the way the rest of society seems to choose to be liberal and fashionable. Truth ... a sense of reality untainted by technical jargon, untouched by scientific problem-solving, but basic, fundamental, humourous in its own contradictory way ... truth ...

I was moved to write about this, moved to create, inspired by roots, inspired by the people the textbooks and imagery of society had taught me were worthless dirty savages.

The Spectre of my Father ...

Transmitting a Vision ...

Throughout this whole period, there had been one source for me of wholeness and example ... a man who had dreams, had wisdom, had his flights of fantasy and silliness ... had, for want of the right word ... humanity.

At ten, in Antwerp, Belgium he had taken me through a convent he helped to guard as part of the occupying forces. Late one Saturday night, by flashlight, we toured the many vaulted rooms. The convent was the storehouse of artworks that had been pillaged in the Second World War — they were being researched to find true ownership before they were returned. By flickering light I saw Rembrandts, Van Goghs, Michelangelos, Renoirs — sculptures, visual art that whispered and beckoned across the centuries — flung ideas and values and beauty to me from voices and minds long gone.

How could I do this — how could I be part of this — how could I project myself to my children's children's children's children's children's children's children?

Introducing the Way ...

At other times my father took me into the bush — showed me the earth, the sky, the animals, talked of the weaving of these into the same fabric in which we, as human beings, were mere threads. All is important, he said. To understand these things is to understand both the large and the small he said, and that this is what we must do — understand, respect and appreciate all natural things and beings.

He did not talk often about these things, but it was there, in everything he did. It was there in his *way.*

The Humanization of my father ...

As I grew older, I found my father, like other human beings, was, after all, only human ...

He didn't like cats. He thought them to be useless pets, giving nothing back: fetching no slippers, providing no welcome home, no companionship, except around feeding time. I saw, too, that somewhere along the line the assimilation promoted by military life had taken its toll. As I became more and more involved in Aboriginal issues and community development, his statements of "Indians are a conquered people, and, as such, are being treated very well" began to chink at that armour of purity I had dressed him in.

There were other things, too, that smacked of his service background: a not-quite-overt racism that labelled enemies, often by colour, creed and place of origin. I began to see that somehow, this man who had taught me to be fair and open-minded, was expecting more in this area from me than from himself.

To begin with, these were negative things. The heart that had once soared with respect for his goodness, was changing from blind adoration to critical appraisal of his ideas and opinions. The heart was still warm, but beginning to see.

We enter the learning curve ...

In retrospect, now, I see my father was actually challenging me: he did not want to be as he was. He knew he was not as he once was. He wanted to return to his own ideal of himself, yet could not take that journey unguided.

By the time my own children were teenagers, it seemed that my father and I had a learning pact: he would teach me the things I did not know or understand well. I would teach him to look, once more, through younger eyes and with vision less jaded.

I hope I learned as well as he did. The years passed with him tinkering and speaking in parables. He had many stories, vibrant and some of immense humour. He had war stories, stories of courage, stories of the old days. He talked, tinkered, invented, drank and listened.

We finally drank together, and then we both stopped. Stopped dead or near to it, and I stayed stopped. He watched me in the painful process of early recovery, watched as I tried to put back on some of the ninety pounds lost in a blur (I've been very successful!!). Watched as I regained, bit by bit, emotional strength.

My father saw my strength grow into joyousness, and set down his last drink for three years. Then the two of us tackled things that needed doing, whether it was recovery for ourselves, our family, or undertaking community doings. We had somehow, without too many words at all, arrived at the same space.

And, that's the way it was from '87 to '90. Major indicator: cats. In '87 my son got a cat. He named her Jim. Now, Jim is a kick-ass cat. She invariably bites the hand that feeds her. She's a mean momma — tuna-addicted, rude and belligerent. To people.

Watching this cat is quite the experience. She's a walking and clawing ethics animation machine. She taught me this: if one only treats with respect and kindness those who can confer a benefit (in this case, tuna) that respect is conditional and is of little value. Jim spends a lot of time dragging in other cats: she offers them all the tuna she can snarl out of us. These cats are invariably smaller than Jim, some are downright mangy. She has fattened up many a streetcat in her day and has often gone tuna-less herself.

These mangy, scrawny cats can confer no benefit on Jim. They often cannot find a warm place to sleep. They most certainly cannot return the dinner invitation.

Jim is invariably kind and helpful to these critters. Seldom to us. I watch her and I think: is this not a true spiritual principle in action? Not to be respectful only for reward, not to be helpful only to help yourself, but to be these things especially in situations where neither occurs.

Dad saw this, too. I would often catch him puzzling over her—she was breaking all his acceptable pet rules. He would watch and think.

Calico Catalyst

Dad, tinkerer and collector of junk, could not resist any and all yard sales. One day, he returned with a prize: an enormous calico cat. It was a floral pink print with a massive satin bow and stuffed to the hilt. I thought he had bought it for my daughter or myself.

"No," he said, "this is mine."

It was one of a very few material territorialism statements I had ever heard from him. And, it was so. Wherever my father travelled, the calico cat was there, stuffed in suitcase, lounging on the back seat of the car, lying in the toolbox.

Two years after his death, I still have it. I still have Jim, too, but that's another story ... by the way, donations of tuna (packed in water only—Jim only serves the finest!) are gratefully accepted.

Dad, after all, really liked cats.

Mother Tongue/Father Tongue

In 1987 I worked as an editor of Aboriginal literature, and it was mighty scarce at that time — there was virtually no work in Aboriginal languages available anywhere, and our languages were dying ...

I wrote many papers about this, developed a methodology for community-based book production, and, at a conference presented one of my works. But my presence there was more important in what I heard than what I gave.

A Navajo speaker talked of Mother Tongue — talked of this as the words of a language. This speaker also talked about Father Tongue — the non-verbal parts of language that we see in actions and body language ...

English as a Different Value System

Working with languages helped me learn many things — understanding the structure of English and its noun-predominance freed me to begin to understand the materialistic influence of the people surrounding me. When one is immersed in a language that primarily gears our thoughts to *things,* we become trapped in a value system of materialism ...

As an Aboriginal writer, I set out on many excursions to find the thing lacking in linear English: the visual texture of so many of the experiences, personal and real, popular and ethereal, that trigger the feeling of oneness with the reader, the feeling of occupying the same eyes and ears of the one experiencing the story — these things I find so elusive in the literary hierarchy of beginning, middle and end. The elusiveness stems from the construction of English: it is a noun-based language with immense material vocabulary, but it is poor in its content of verbs, adjectives and adverbs. Both the linear structure of the language and the formulae developed to use it, restrict the ability of a writer to express emotion, relationships, texture and depth, unless, of course, one deals with *things* instead of *people.*

English with other Value Applications ...

So, I tampered with what I had: a real need to express and

access words that could conjure and replicate feelings and ideas. I explored my cultural roots, my people's languages, I explored a different way of looking at life, concurrent, as opposed to linear. Verbs, adjectives, adverbs replacing nouns, movement and time-motion relationships replacing rigid technical formulae.

In 1989 I had lunch with a friend who speaks and reads Ukrainian. Ukrainian is a language of about thirty-five thousand words, each sound represented by a cyrhillic symbol. He looked at the menu and said: "I can tell by the silent letters and the number of words on this menu that English speakers have more than they need ..."

What a concept — we were constantly told that one reason why our languages weren't practical was because there weren't enough words ... but do you really need words for things you don't need?

Yet in other ways Aboriginal languages are both practical and rich ... in 1990 I went four hundred miles North of the Arctic Circle and asked the Inuit that favourite question ... why do you have so many words for snow? There is only one type of snow you can make an icehouse out of, they said, and this is survival ...

And, as I continued to work with Aboriginal languages, other questions arose and were answered ...

Why do Aboriginal languages give a Proper Name to a living tree? because it is a friend, a peer, and just as important as you or I ...

Why are Aboriginal languages rich with verbs, adverbs, adjectives? they are not materialistic, but movement and relationship-oriented ...

Now, I thought, somehow, my father, in English could transmit these things. Was it the way he told his stories? was it his vocabulary? Was it how he used stories themselves as analogous examples? Was it the unpredictable and sometimes confusing structures and structurelessness? Was it how, in the process of analogy that transferability of teachings occur? Yes, yes to all.

And other soft sciences ...

As I charged about my life, I decided it was high time that I learned a little technical stuff about Aboriginal origins and signed up for yet another course — this one in Anthropology. I've always had the problem of not being able to curb my curiosity ...

The more I learned, the more I read, the course requirements were long since finished and I was still haunting libraries, yard sales, Sally Ann's, for more and more Anthro-junk. It was kind of like popcorn, never satisfying, as I never found a convincing sense of self in these writings, but, certain little scraps were leaking into me and setting up a domino effect.

One of the most enlightening scraps was labelled "pseudo-speciation." This is a process used to desensitize us, to make the enemy less-than-human in our eyes. For example, if, instead of seeing human beings rush us in war, we see a sub-species called "Gooks" or "Krauts," (please excuse), we can then convince ourselves that we are not really murdering with our own hands other human beings. Pseudo-speciation is not only used in times of war, but in times of peace to control social structure, promote racism and sexism, colonize territory, obliterate opposition and promote fascism.

The most profound and insidious form of pseudo-speciation today is contrived through statistical reporting. A listing of six million deaths is too profound for us to understand, we must reject this or our minds will literally boggle. We become desensitized by statistical proliferation, no faces or human characteristics are assigned in the numbers. We see no families, no value systems, no aspirations. We somehow begin to believe that those six million deserved it.

Pseudo-speciation has two effects: it dehumanizes the victims of gross atrocities, but its lasting impact is on the spirits of the millions who read about such things and dismiss them. These people become dehumanized through the loss of compassion. Their souls become torn; innocence is lost.

If an Aboriginal person is not seen as a human being, it is easy to deny rights. It is easy to allow us to die thirty years ahead of the rest of the population.

Yet, if we can show compassion and understanding for one human being, if we feel we can know them and like them, then in the caring that circles, the statistics can be changed from the bottom up. For this reason I want you to get to know me through my work, I would get to know you, if I could. Let me. Maybe we could begin to understand cats ... in reading these things, my father demystified before me ... but there's one more story about him yet ...

NO BOXES FOR ME

In writing "Fencepost Sitting and How I Fell Off to One Side," there were several factors that contributed to the style I developed and used:

1. In March 1990, I was asked by *Artscraft Magazine* to write an article for them on appropriation of Aboriginal ideas and stories. Due to the fact that many of my articles had appeared in their magazine previously, they agreed to publish it, sight unseen before submission.

2. For several years I had been storymaking and storytelling, and often enjoyed the rapport with people that is established when we really let them see us as we really are.

3. I had participated in and observed my own life and people around me and realized that although we are trained to think of time as a linear thing, it is only linear if one does not recognize that concurrences occur: while I am doing X, someone who affects my life may be doing Y. There are times when these incidents come together like scattered buffalo to form a rumbling herd.

4. If I believe in a continuum, the Circle, then I don't have to opt in at the Beginning, muddle through the Middle, and

be victimized by the End. I can join the Circle at any time, in any place.

5. Holographs have always fascinated me: they say that if you break one, any of the parts include the whole image. Much harder to do with writing, but I thought I would like to try it — Aboriginal value systems demand to be wholly expressed.

6. I had spent many years in social work, dealing with statistics, trends, politicians. It never ceased to amaze me that one could quote statistics of Indians: lowest life expectancy, numbers before the Invasion and after, percentage of prison enrollment, etc. and nothing would get done. These numbers allowed us to be faceless and impersonal, not real and warm, someone or a people that others could care about, if they could get by their own racism.

7. That racism is a symptom of a kind of thinking, a thinking that allows hierarchy to govern and injustice to prevail. I am committed in my work to address that hierarchy, to destabilize the kind of thinking that it generates.

8. When my spirit re-enters this plane, I hope I don't come back as a herd animal. Not because I don't like our Brothers and Sisters, but because I like them best one or two at a time. This way I can get to know them, know their struggles and solutions, know their discord and how they find peace. I thought, maybe, others may feel this way — dare I risk letting people know me?

The Way of my Work and the Four Ripples

I see myself at the centre of four ripples in a pool. The first thing I write for is to express myself, for myself. I write because I can't help it.

The second ripple represents the Aboriginal community: if somehow I can communicate and connect with my own people, I have met the responsibility of this second ripple.

The third ripple is the larger community: that which victimizes us, controls our environment, and, at times, our thoughts. If in some way I can change some attitudes "out there" through my work, I have fulfilled the responsibility of the third ripple.

The fourth ripple is Honoured, I believe, by meeting the other three. This is the most important. By meeting the other three, I believe I have shown gratitude to the Creator. Have in some way, fulfilled my responsibility.

My Father

Dad was a Cree and a career army man. He left the services after the Second World War for a rousing boxing career. The new career lasted forty-five seconds. In his first and only professional bout, his nose was almost literally put behind his left ear with the first landed punch. He then returned to pioneer farming, but could not scratch out a living for us. Back to the armed services he went for the next twenty years.

Dad was streamed, I guess. He was good with his hands and became a tradesman. The training that he undertook changed his life.

To teach him welding, they sealed him in a lead box with a welding torch and gas tubes. He had to use the right mix of gases for the composition of the metal and cut himself out before all the oxygen was used up. He did it, of course, but until his death in 1990, he would still, when in his cups, relive the terror of the darkness, the isolation. This strong man, this proud and sensitive man, they put him in a box.

It took a cat to get him out of there. A cat for my Dad to understand and examine his own manipulation by colonization.

No boxes for me.

Joy Asham Fedorick

Joy Asham Fedorick is a storyteller, cultural commentator, and playwright who has published in periodicals and newspapers for twenty years. She is the author of *Language Without Refuge*, a book on the disappearance of Aboriginal languages published by the Ojibway/Cree Cultural Centre, Timmins, Ontario.

Fedorick was the founder and director of *Earthtones North*, a large-scale project addressing Aboriginal language retention through literature development and community-based book production in far northern reserve communities.

In 1992 she co-authored a multi-media performance collaboration with Ted Harasymchuk, Ukrainian-Canadian Tsymbalist. The performance, titled *Salt and Sage*, is about finding common ground, balance and cooperation across cultures. She increasingly presents her writing through installation and site-specific work. In the summer of 1992 she collaborated with Kil-Young Yoo on a mixed-media installation for *A Space* Artists' Centre in Toronto.

Fedorick has taught creative writing and aboriginal values in Toronto high schools and acted as a resource person for graduate students at York University. She continues to work in desktop publishing, and she also teaches desk-top publishing on a contract basis.

In addition to her creative work, Fedorick is a community activist. She began the Ontario Women's Directorate Northern Office in Thunder Bay and headed it for six years. She has extensive community development experience in the core area of Winnipeg, Manitoba, where she developed alternative education programs and worked with children, youth, and women.

Fedorick is the coordinator of *Full Screen*, an independent film and video collective of First Nations artists and artists of colour.

Give Back
by *Jaune Quick-To-See Smith*

Jaune Quick-To-See Smith, *Buffalo,* 1992, oil, collage, mixed media on canvas,
diptych 66 × 96, photo: Scott Bowron, courtesty Steinbaum/Krauss Gallery, NY

Jaune Quick-to-See Smith, photo courtesy Steinbaum/Krauss Gallery

This speech was the conference keynote address at the Women's Caucus for Art 1992 National Conference.

By all odds, I should not be here today. In 1940 when I was born, one in ten Indian children survived. I grew up with a nomadic, illiterate father, moving from reservation to reservation. **By all odds, I should not be here today.** As a child, I knew hunger, welfare homes, and living in one-room cabins. When only one Indian in 5000 of my age attains an advanced degree, **I should not be here today.** And yet, for many Indians with college degrees, my story is not remarkable.

1992 has become a focal point, a benchmark, a year of dissension, with chaos around the world, pronouncement of a hole in the ozone layer over the northern hemisphere, governments crumbling, countries rebuilding, more homeless in America, more mediocrity in our leadership, world populations swelling beyond global capacity, and America is gearing up to spend billions to celebrate its discovery myth.

1992 is also a focal point for American Indians. More of our history is being revised, reassessed and rewritten, so I don't want to give you a laundry list of recriminations. I simply want to refute three major myths that our public schools have promoted.

Myth Number One: American Indians had no written language. We had a variety of written languages and the greatest, the Mayan, when it was burned by the Spanish, was housed in a library equal to the library in Alexandria.

Myth Number Two: American Indians had no wheel. We had a wheel; in fact I am working on a public art project with the Duwamish people of Seattle to rebuild a six-foot water wheel which was an automatic fishing machine.

Myth Number Three: The American continent was an empty wilderness with a few savages wandering around. We had vast populations, estimated at fifty to eighty million in

1492, calculated to be equal to that of Europe at the time. There were great cities and architecture that equalled and rivalled Europe and Egypt together, with knowledge that exceeded Europe and Egypt in medicine, math, botany and some areas of the arts such as weaving.

The terms "New World" and "Old World" are from a Eurocentric viewpoint. Both worlds arose along a similar time line but with two major differences. The first is that Indian people governed themselves in a sharing environment, believing that *no one* person or group of people owned the land, the water or the sky and yet, that each was responsible for the use of that environment. Secondly, with an all encompassing reverence for nature they maintained the ecosystem across the North and South American continents. Today, the industrial world's mismanagement of the environment has led scientists around the world to seek out and research indigenous people's knowledge — farming in the desert without irrigation, farming inside the rainforest without disturbing the ecosystem — and their vast knowledge of the medicinal properties of plants. These are samples of desperately needed science for today's world.

For 1992 I have two challenges that I would like to put forth:

First, for 1992, I challenge this audience to expand the goals of the academic art community and begin in earnest to research and write about the Americas.

H. W. Janson's *History of Art* is a sexist, racist view of history. We have the knowledge, wisdom, talent and ability right in this room to write a history of art which is inclusive, not exclusive. Look at the synoptic tables in the back of his book. He leaves out three-quarters of the world's contribution to art in his European time line. To put things into perspective, please read the book *Black Athena,*

Jack Weatherford's *Indian Givers* and *Native Roots,* and Lucy Lippard's *Mixed Blessings.* I encourage you to write this history, because women are traditionally the nurturers, recorders of stories, and peacemakers in most societies. Women need to recoup these abilities and use them in an invasive way to affect the art world, education and politics in this country.

Researching and recording the history of the Americas is a major task that needs to be done. We know more about the pyramids of Egypt than the pyramids of America, which were larger. We know more about the weavings of Europe than the weavings of the Americas, which have never been duplicated anywhere. Some of the finest sculpture, jewelry, goldwork has been done in the Americas and has had very little written about it and yet has had an impact on the modern architecture of this country.

Polly Schaafsma and Campbell Grant have researched and recorded a few specific areas of rock art in the West and Southwest, but Grant notes that there are really few areas in North America that have been thoroughly recorded or studied.

Nor have there been any penetrating studies of the movements and extreme intermixing of styles that occurred throughout North America and around the world. For example, there is an intricate maze symbol that appears on a seventh-century B.C. Etruscan vase, in the Italian Alps, and on a coin from Crete. It is repeated line for line on a massive block of granite in the Wicklow mountains in Ireland — carved on a ledge in Cornwall; it's found again in Nayarit, Mexico and the Galisteo Basin, New Mexico — again in Oraibi, Arizona, and on today's modern Pima basketry. How is it that this glyph symbol appears in these scattered and remote areas and across continents? There are enough mysteries to occupy scientists, historians, and archaeologists for the next five hundred years.

In writing this history of the Americas, we need to do two important things. *Listen to our elders. Use teamwork.*

As people of colour, we honour our elders; we record

their stories; we seek their wisdom. Our Indian tribal colleges are including the elders in our curriculum; they are teaching classes on botany, Indian medicine, traditional foods, hide tanning, beadwork, crafts, tipi building, storytelling, handsigning and language.

In the mainstream of community, I don't see the same search for knowledge from the elders. Faith Ringgold is an elder. She has lived in Harlem all her life and has developed her work from her community and her mother. Faith is a role model and she has made her work against economic constraints and discrimination. Miriam Schapiro is an elder and a role model for all women. For over thirty years she has traversed the United States, meeting with women, giving them words of support and encouragement for their art. I've been to small colleges in Idaho, Montana, Iowa, Minnesota, Arizona, Oklahoma, Nebraska, Kansas and found women who spoke of her as a mentor. Her dedicated work affected a generation of women, and men as well. Lucy Lippard is an elder. She has changed the face of art writing in New York and across the continent. Always one step ahead, she began interacting with the communities of artists of colour over fifteen years ago.

What drives these women beyond art world enclaves? Why have they taken a path not trod by others? Their stories are available only in a scant number of catalogues, if at all. They have much to teach us, and we are missing a valuable part of art history in the United States.

Research America by going into the field, not the library shelves, or archives or storage. Do your research first hand.

We also need to have *teamwork*. With the current budget cuts, we are going to suffer from lack of funds. In the Indian world, our survival mechanism has been to share. Our twenty-six tribal colleges share grants, share books, share teachers, share resources. At Salish Kootenai College, our book budget has been three hundred dollars per year for all books — science, forestry, biology, math, etcetera. Between my book drives at universities (when I go to speak) and our librarian scrounging for remaindered books across the nation, we now have the largest library of all the tribal colleges. We truck books to Indians in prison; we truck books to the six tribal colleges in Montana and five community centres across our reservation. *Teamwork.* One university could write this piece, another university could write that piece. *Teamwork will get the job done.*

This audience could create a new time line of art and write a new book of art history. We can stand around and criticize H.W. Janson or we can do something about it.

Moira Roth developed a slide file and film department on Women Artists of Colour. There is a dire need for this information. Faith Ringgold conducted a survey on Artists of Colour; it's on disc and waits at this moment for funds to print it and distribute it to universities, museums, and art groups across the country. Gail Tremblay, an Iroquois professor at Evergreen College, has compiled a computer list of Indian artists from across the nation. You can help expand and increase knowledge in the art world by participating. As a team you could create a new time line which would affect art and art history departments immediately.

My first challenge is to write the history of the Americas into the world of art.

I have a second challenge for 1992. Recycle your academic writing.

Write, not just for your academic community, not just for the art elite, but for a broader audience. Recycle your writing. Bring art out of the closet. Make it available to the mainstream. Make art visible to the public. Help educate the masses. Teach people that art tells us who we are. Art defines society. Art enhances life. Recycle your writing and heighten awareness; raise consciousness. Help us get more support in congress. Bring art to the schools and the supermarket. Educate the public. In the Indian world we say, "Do it for the children."

Mainstream Americans are questioning their traditions.

They are changing their views about conquering and destroying the environment and looking to the Native communities for answers. They are questioning their traditional Judeo-Christian religions and creating new age philosophies from American Indian, African and Asian religions.

They are changing their views about global politics and thinking about common markets and world technology. New paradigms are needed. Think of yourself as a shaper of new paradigms.

1. Think of yourself as a **bridge** between your community, the mainstream, as well as ethnic communities. We should be equally at home with academics, business people, people of colour, or politicians — their systems and institutions. We need to be visible in sharing information about art.

2. Think of yourself as **orator, speaker, translator and educator** outside the academic community.

3. Think of yourself as a **networker** who does consciousness-raising about the arts in your local public schools, libraries, and the business community. Reach outside the university and the arts community.

4. Think of yourself as a **role model**, whether you organize, direct, nurture or expand arts awareness in your local community.

5. Think of yourself as a **writer**, not just for the academic community but for popular magazines, airline magazines, business magazines, and local papers.

6. Think of yourself as a **politician**. We can't be afraid to be seen as racist or radical. We do have to encourage ethnic peoples to contribute to our art departments, our local museums, and American society. We learn more about ourselves in sharing and expanding our knowledge and yes, in comparing our differences.

7. Think of yourself as the **catalyst** that creates the

ripples and then the waves — that everything you exhibit, everything you write, every place you travel — will touch one — then two — then more.

8. Think of yourself as a **mentor**. Mentor a student or provide a scholarship or team up to provide a scholarship.

In the Indian world we say, "Give back." Martin Luther King said "Identify with the underprivileged. Identify with those who have been left out of the sunlight of opportunity."

Think of yourself as a bridge, a networker, a role model, a mentor and a team worker. Give Back.

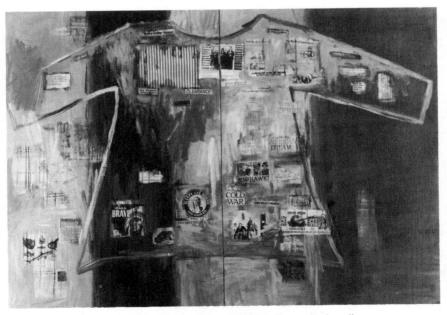

Jaune Quick-To-See Smith, *War Shirt*, 1992, oil, collage, mixed-media on canvas, diptych, 60" × 84", photo: Scott Bowron, courtesty Steinbaum/Krauss Gallery, New York

69

Jaune Quick-to-See Smith, *Target*, oil, collage, mixed-media on canvas, diptych, 112" × 42"

right: *The Red Mean: Self-Portrait*, oil, collage, mixed-meadia on canvas, diptych 90" × 60"

photos: Scott Bowron, courtesty Steinbaum/Krauss Gallery, New York

Jaune Quick-to-See Smith

Jaune Quick-to-See Smith got her name from her Shoshone grandmother. Born in Montana, she was one of eleven children raised on the Flathead reservation by her father, Arthur Smith, a horseman, rodeo rider, and trader.

Smith knew she wanted to be an artist from an early age. At ten, she used money she earned working as a farm hand after school to send away for the "Famous Artists" mail order course. Determined to go to college, she left Montana and worked at part-time jobs while studying in Boston, Seattle, Houston and New Mexico. In 1982, when she was already a well-known artist and forty-two years old, Smith received a Masters degree from the University of New Mexico.

Smith now lives on the outskirts of Corrales, New Mexico. Between her numerous engagements speaking and teaching throughout the United States and internationally, she paints in a converted stable, with her horse Cheyenne for company.

Smith has founded two artists' cooperatives: the Coup Marks on the Flathead Reserve and the Gray Canyon Artists in Albuquerque. Among the many shows she has curated are *Our Land/Ourselves: Contemporary Native American Landscape*, for the State University of New York, and *The Submuloc Show or the Columbus Wohs,* featuring thirty-five Native Americans. She has just completed curating and writing the catalogue for an exhibit featuring twenty-seven First Nations contemporary artists, *We the Human Beings*, for Wooster College, Ohio.

Smith lectures and works as a visiting artist at colleges and universities throughout the United States. She has been the subject of three PBS films, as well as German and Finnish documentaries.

Racism:
Racial Exclusivity
and Cultural Supremacy

by Jeannette Armstrong

Jeannette Armstrong, photo: Gregg Young-Ing

My intent is to call upon the integrity of our common human spirit in these words that I share with you. It is not my intent to belabour a past steeped in racist doctrine but rather to speak of the present and the future. In doing so, it is my hope that I might assist in the bringing about of better understanding in the questions this organization ponders in the task to which the *Committee to Combat Racism* has been set.

I speak from my individual experience as an indigenous North American person in a society dominated by Euro-Western thought. As such, I come here to share my thinking on these matters towards positive change. I began my talk in my language to draw attention to language and the difficulty in usage of words. It is often assumed that if one speaks the same language, words have the same meaning. As I am a crafter of words this is where my talk shall find its focus. For albeit, I speak English to you, rather than my own language, I might as well speak my language, because the meanings of the English words I use arise out of my Okanagan understanding of the world.

Words have meanings which we take for granted when we speak in a given language. I use the example of a word, of which we may be commonly familiar, if we speak English. The word *tree* conjures up an image that we may think has the same meaning, but let us consider a few meanings and how they might arise.

A general image of a "tree" might emerge out of the layers of images of all the possible trees and illustrations of trees that we each have encountered. Each of us might therefore share a kind of sensory composite, symbolic of trees in general for recognition purposes. The meaning that trees have to each of us, however, seems to be bound up in how we each relate to trees.

To someone from the lumber or paper industry, the word *tree* has a significantly different meaning than to an orchardist. Likewise, a person from the Arctic circle will have a profoundly different meaning gathered from TV and book illustrations, than a person from the rain forest. A person who has never walked under trees in forests and heard breezes rustling through leaves as birds filled branches, filtering sunlight and rain, will never truly know a tree. To the person whose direct survival depends on trees, the *tree* has a deeper cultural meaning—steeped in an essence of gratitude toward the creation of the tree, and therefore enveloped within a unique cultural expression of reverence toward creation.

In this light, consider the extreme difference between a logging conglomerate president's meaning and one in whose culture *trees* are living relatives in spirit, though the word might be referred to, by both, in English. Can we say that these are two different trees? Or might it be possible to understand that this is only one tree that has two different meanings?

Words have a covering of meaning derived from unique relationships to things, beyond the generally accepted descriptive sensory symbol. Thousands of generations of relating to things in a given way give rise to cultural meaning attached to words. Thus, even though I might translate *tree* into an English word, my cultural meaning remains intact as though spoken in my language while your cultural understanding of the word remains locked within the context of your culture. Unless you also speak my language, or permit me to fully interpret my meaning, the *tree* of which I speak remains a *tree* cloaked in my culture and language which excludes my meaning.

Words, in being shaped through language emerging out of culture, have a rootedness in meaning which renders them exclusionary. My very real situation is that I am here speaking not my language to you, and in doing so, realize that it is I who must frame my thinking into another language. A language which excludes all of my Okanagan cultural understanding as though it were non-existent. In so doing I also realize that you and I will likely remain in this position, and as long as this is so, racism will continue.

Herein lies a dilemma which presents itself to illustrate the problem that I have been asked to address at this consultation. My words to you can only be a glimpse into an immense forest of similar trees, that we need to share each other's views on, in order to begin the task of understanding the nature of racism. I offer my thoughts on words to bridge into my understanding of the culturally exclusionary nature of racism.

Words seem to be standardized out of common experience and therefore out of the common thought of a people. The unique ability to retain and recount common understanding of the hows and the whys of the doing of things, important to survival, emerges in the expressive arts.

Spoken language is only one system of expression. One which is least dependent upon anything outside of the human body and most efficient in not interfering with other activities of the body. Spoken language, therefore, has developed the largest vocabulary of symbols which represent understanding. One does not have to drag in an uprooted tree or take everyone outdoors and point out a tree to communicate about a tree. Nor does one need to stop what one is doing to act out or draw a tree shape. One only makes sounds and relies on the mutual recognition of words to be understood.

Spoken language, then, is one system which signifies meaning and therefore contains thought. Many other complex systems of expression carry cultural meaning which cannot be expressed in words. Music, visual arts, dance and performance are but a few that are similar across cultures. Expressive arts can thus be seen as symbols devised to transmit ways of thinking and ways of doing things. The ways of thinking and the ways of doing things being a process of everyday life experience.

In this way, culture can be seen as a process, and language can be seen as one of the receptacles and vehicles by which the process is shaped, transmitted and learned. Through the transmission of thought embedded in cultural process, human action and interaction and its resultant outcomes takes place. Language plays a powerful role in information transmitted as a carrier of thought or a world view of a people. The thought or the world view, however, is the shaper of cultural process.

Peoples bound together through culture process become disposed to culture blindness and become culture centric. Things do not make sense unless somehow translated into a context which has meaning within the cultural process. Culture centricity becomes entrenched as tradition, through underlying structures which reinforce the world view, because they reinforce stability and continuance. Continuance is assured in the methods used to teach cultural process to ensuing generations.

All peoples have evolved cultural processes to teach and maintain world view. Education, church and media are examples. The innate disposition of such processes are culture centric. In and of itself, culture centricity can be seen as tradition and a stabilizing element in cultural process. If it works and has always worked then it is taught to the young as the only way to do things to make sure they survive. Values arise out of cultural processes and are transferred to the succeeding generations.

Culture centricity evolves into ethnocentricity when groups with similar cultural processes associate over generations and reinforce a wider centricity that encompasses racial types. A status quo becomes established as large numbers enjoin a common tradition through cultural process. Such an evolvement is not necessarily damaging if adjustments are made, slowly allowing reciprocal learning and securing enrichment and growth in each culture.

Racism occurs as racially related cultural groups act in concert to validate and insure for themselves an ethnocentric view to the exclusion of another racial or cultural group. Racism entrenches itself through coercive acts devised to suppress and replace the culture of other peoples. Racism as such is no more than cultural imperialism arising out of an inability to overcome ethnocentrically disposed views maintained out of tradition.

Racism might then be seen as a form of cultural rigidity, characterized by a cultural blindness to all its own processes. An inability, so to speak, to perceive knowledge outside of the narrow limits of a culture bound racial type. A refusal to enrich and grow beyond one view of the world. This might lead one to refuse to see a tree as more than a commodity because accumulation of material wealth might have been once a necessary tradition of survival, in a culture where material wealth was restricted only to an elite. Even though conditions might change and there could be enough for everyone, a person of such a culture might devise many justifications to continue to enforce such traditions without understanding why such processes may no longer be necessary, beneficial or intelligent.

Racism becomes a destructive force of cultural supremacy in its abject justification of aggressive ethnocentricity. There can be no doubt that racism is a destructive force if one racial type can act in concert to justify conquest and subjugation of another racial type towards genocide. There can be no doubt that cultural supremacy is a racially destructive force if continued oppression means continued deaths to a people. Cultural imperialism, whether by physical means or purely psychological means, achieves the same destructive ends — even while such cultural blindness might be perceived from inside only as a necessity to bring to knowledge those who are perceived to have no knowledge of their own.

Peoples whose cultural processes and world view might not allow, or conceive of coercion and conquest are defenseless against such cultural intolerance. Conquest of such cultural groups is easily achieved through aggression and domination. Fear, ignorance and arrogance fuel overt aggression when one culture, which might have no knowledge of the principles of co-existence and cooperation, comes into contact with another culture which practices those principles and expects them to be maintained.

Such culturally supremacist racism could then justify countless inhumane measures of conquest — including massive military annihilation, enslavement and control — under the guise of civilization. Once coercion has been exerted to the point of subjugation, control is enforced through the functions of society which transmit culture. Continued attempts to force acceptance of principles which are culturally reprehensible results in psychological oppression and an internalized spiritual disintegration. The death rate of my peoples here in North America, no less than in other colonized countries where physical force is used, continues to rise without gunfire.

Freedom of religion does not mean freedom of thought and absolutely excludes freedom of choice, when people are ordered to submit their children to the hands of another culture for educational and religious instruction to the utter exclusion of their teachings. Nor is it any different when the power to choose is removed through economic and legal control. Refusal to understand the true nature of oppression may make guilt easier to bear because there are no bloody corpses. But death is the same, whatever the means. It may be easier to shrug off the guilt by perceiving cultural resistance to be racial inferiority, simply requiring the oppressing culture to enforce better opportunity to participate in so-called "human experience."

When agressive conquest takes place, perhaps a greater tragedy than the mass deaths of individuals is the irreplaceable loss of cultural knowledge and the resultant loss of the opportunity to enrich human interaction.

Cultural supremacy, cultural imperialism and cultural exclusivity are words we need to examine when we say racism. Cultural processes devised to perpetuate an ethnocentric world view must be seen in the light of racial aggression. Let there be no doubt that they are tools of aggression — as long as they remain culturally oppressive and exclusionary and as long as people are dying as a result. If there is to be an examination and a questing for knowledge, which will help humanity to transcend racism, there must be a striving to rise above ethnocentric aggression and cultural supremacy. I shall not isolate education, church and media as the only tools, except to say that those tools are perhaps more subtle and insidious because they are at the centre of perpetuating, preserving and justifying Euro-Western thought.

If we see racism in this light then we can see attempts to wipe out differences as a denial of cultural relevance outside of the cultures dominating through conquest. We can then see cultural intolerance for what it is. We can then see education, media and the church in the light of cultural processes, which by their nature are ethnocentrically disposed, and which by historical practice are culturally supremacist and suppressive as intrinsically racist institutions in and of themselves. In light of these observations I ask a question that you may not choose to ask of yourselves. When you set out to combat racism, what is your goal? Do you mean that your task is to find better ways to assimilate others into your world view?

A question which you might ask yourselves is: What fuels conquest? What is the central driving force contained within the nature of aggression? How does it manifest itself as a cultural value which can allow subjugation, exploitation and continued oppression?

Perhaps it is not so much the distinction by racial type that is destructive, but the cultural intolerance which insinuates itself as racism. Cultural intolerance manifests itself as a psychologically destructive force that only the culturally oppressed can articulate. Perhaps it is exclusionary aggression under the guise of progress and civilization which masks itself in the social-cultural processes of education, media and the church. Perhaps this aggression eats away like a cancer at our attempts at co-existence as humans and our co-existence with other life forms on this earth.

Perhaps it is a time to examine the nature of tolerance and true respect for differences. Perhaps it is a time to be courageous enough to examine ethnocentric ignorance and cultural blindness manifested within cultural institutions. Perhaps it is a time to see that, regardless of number, all branches from one tree are dependent on the whole tree for life. Perhaps it is a time to learn new meanings and new words.

The larger question that I bring you is this: Might racism be a symptom of a deeper, more damaging disease to humanity and to the Earth? My question relates to intolerance. And, perhaps deeper than intolerance, my question relates to the basic and fundamental values which allow aggression and domination to occur. It relates to the exclusionary measures which are commonly expressed as racism. My question relates to the nature of the concept of supremacy, a perceived prior right above others and other life forms. My question relates to the possibility of tolerance, harmony and cooperation. My question relates to the condition of trees and the condition of humanity at this time. Perhaps it is a time to nourish the great tree of peace that our peoples have been shown, so that its roots might spread outward to all lands and its branches to shelter all life.

Perhaps if these questions can be examined honestly, then we might begin the work of building understanding, respect and love among each other toward a better future. Perhaps it is in that future that we will reach our full potential as thinking creatures. Creatures whose sacred gift is the power to manifest thought and therefore change its external world. Creatures whose task it is to learn to use those gifts to live and continue rather than to conquer, destroy and perish. Perhaps it is time to learn to appreciate and to love creation. Perhaps it is a time for knowledge. Perhaps it is a time to learn the meaning of trees.

Jeannette Armstrong

Jeannette Armstrong is an Okanagan Indian. She is a fluent speaker of the Okanagan language, and she has studied traditional teachings and practiced traditional ways for many years under the direction of Okanagan Elders.

She is a writer, sculptor, artist, teacher, and an outspoken Aboriginal Rights activist.

After studying Creative Writing and receiving a degree in Fine Arts through the University of Victoria, she focused her work toward developing First Nations Educational Institutions. She is founder and former Director of En'owkin Centre and is currently the Director of En'owkin International Writing School. Armstrong is committed to the development of literature and the arts among First Nations people and the realization and promotion of the distinct artistic forms of First Nations people as viable and acceptable in the international arts and literary community.

Armstrong has written a number of books including *Slash,* a novel, *Breathtracks,* a collection of poetry, and several children's books as well as various film scripts produced for television. Her collaborations with other First Nations poets and musicians have also appeared on several tapes and CDs including "Till the Bars Break."

She recently co-authored, with renowned architect Douglas Cardinal, *The Native Creative Process* (Penticton: Theytus Books, 1992).

Armstrong's commitment to the development of Native creative expression and the de-colonization of First Nations has been articulated in a number of her articles, lectures and workshops over the years. Her ability to grasp the unique process of creative expression among Native artists and her astute insight into social and political issues is well-known and respected among First Nations People.

Oratory:
Coming to Theory

by Lee Maracle

Lee Maracle, photo: Brenda Hemsing

Theory. If it can't be shown, it can't be understood. Theory is a proposition, proven by demonstrable argument. Argument: evidence, proof. Evidence: demonstrable testimony, demonstration. We are already running into trouble. There are a number of words in the English language with no appreciable definition. Argument is defined as evidence; proof or evidence is defined as demonstration or proof; and theory as a proposition proven by demonstrable evidence. None of these words exist outside of their interconnectedness. Each is defined by the other.

Oratory, on the other hand, is unambiguous in its meaning. Oratory: place of prayer, to persuade. This is a word we can work with. We regard words as coming from original being — a sacred spiritual being. The orator is coming from a place of prayer and as such attempts to be persuasive. Words are not objects to be wasted. They represent the accumulated knowledge, cultural values, the vision of an entire people or peoples. We believe the proof of a thing or idea is in the doing. Doing requires some form of social interaction and thus, *story* is the most persuasive and sensible way to present the accumulated thoughts and values of a people.

Among European scholars there is an alienated notion which maintains that theory is separate from story, and thus a different set of words are required to "prove" an idea than to "show" one. Yet if you take the story out of any school textbook the student is left without proof for the positing of any information. In a science textbook they refer to the story as "an example." The component parts of every example are the same: there is a plot line, tension (conflict), a climax and a conclusion. Mathematical "problems" have the same components. The tension in math is one number versus another, whether they are added or subtracted, multiplied or divided, the tension is resolved into some sort of conclusion different from the two numbers representing the original tension. The numbers have names and the plot line (what to do next) is provided by the theorems and formulae which the student accepts by custom. Numbers lack character — human form. But when we propose them as a problem, confronting real people, they take on a character and human content — social interaction. The number of trees cut to make one edition of a newspaper, for example, or the number of hungry children in a large Canadian city.

Academicians waste a great deal of effort deleting character, plot, and story from theoretical arguments. By referring to instances and examples, previous human interaction, and social events, academics convince themselves of their own objectivity and persuade us that the story is no longer a story. However, *our* intellectuals (elders) know that "$E=MC^2$" means nothing outside of human interaction. Likewise, the concept of zero means nothing. It is represented by a circle devoid of all life. This has no meaning for the living or the dead, but it is useful in teaching young children to interact in a positive social fashion. A child learns that if she doesn't obey the laws of the people, she will suffer great nothingness in her interaction with women and men.

Enough of that talk. There is a story in every line of theory, not in our capacity to theorize. It seems a waste of words to dispassionately delete character from plot line, tension, and conclusion. It takes a great deal of work to erase people from theoretical discussion.

A theoretical proposition advanced by John Stuart Mill in his little essay "Utilitarianism" seems the foundation of theory, law, politics, sociology and culture in North America: "All men are motivated by pleasure and pain." John first has to delete his passion from his theory and his life. The great problem with that, of course, is that people think *being* is a passionate thing.

People are extremely disinclined toward celibacy. "the spirit is strong, but the flesh is weak" — so says Jesus. In contrast, we believe that the human spirit and the body agree: to be passionate is to be alive. You cannot erase passion from the spirit of people. At times people can harness their passionate energy and transform it, putting it to work at endeavors other than sexual expression. But to delete passion from our lives leads to a weird kind of sociopathy—a heartlessness.

Next Mr. John Mill had to delete certain types of people, those who regard "pleasure as a physical thing." Now we have a spirit without passion and a mind without a body. Unfortunately, there is not much left to deal with here because the mind is also physical. What is left is a very cold, calculating and dispassionate Mr. J. S. Mill. It takes a lot of work to delete the emotional and passionate self from story, to de-humanize story into "theory." So we don't do it. We humanize theory by fusing humanity's need for common direction—theory—with story.

Finally, not even Mr. Mill is home. What you have left is a calculator with an attitude. No one in the 1990's is going to reduce themselves to a calculator when you can trot over to K-Mart and buy one for less than twenty dollars. We tend to resent uncaring attitudes. So we don't do it. Our orators know that words governing human direction are sacred, prayerful presentations of the human experience, its direction, and the need for transformation in the human condition which arises from time to time.

What is the point of presenting the human condition in a language separate from the human experience: passion, emotion, and character? "If you want people to have confidence in your cure, speak in a language no one understands—Latin. No one speaks Latin anymore, so it is the one we will use." (So said Norman Bethune, delivering a lecture to medical students on medical practice.) By presenting theory in a language no one can grasp, the speaker (or writer) retains authority over thought. By demanding that all thoughts (theory) be presented in this manner in order to be considered theory (thought), the presenter retains the power to make decisions *on behalf of others.*

Recently, there was a conference at Opitsit (Meares Island) to discuss and shape thoughts on the importance of trees to the environment. Native and European environmentalists both attended. The morning consisted of presentations made by "prominent" environmentalists, who droned on about p.b.m.'s, choloform counts, soil erosion, and so forth — none of which was understood by the Native people there. All of our people spoke and understood English, but none had any background in Latin, so the presentations by the environmentalists went over all their heads. At the end, an old man got up and said he would like to give an Indian point of view. Gratefully, the environmentalists bent their ears to listen. The old man spoke for three hours in his language, then sat down.

The Natives cracked up. The environmentalists sat confused.

Unfortunately, the environmentalists missed the point. We all strive to become orators. An orator is simply someone who has come to grips with the human condition, humanity's relationship to creation, and the need for a human direction that will guarantee the peaceful co-existence of human beings with all things under creation. No brilliance exists outside of the ability of human beings to grasp the brilliance and move with it. Thus we *say* what we think. No thought is understood outside of humanity's interaction. So we present thought through story, human beings doing something, real characters working out the process of thought and being.

For Native people, the ridiculousness of European academic notions of theoretical presentation lies in the inherent hierarchy retained by academics, politicians, law makers, and law keepers. Power resides with the theorists so long as they use language no one understands. In order to gain the right to theorize, one must attend their institutions for many years, learn this other language, and unlearn our feeling for the human condition. Bizarre.

If it cannot be shown, it cannot be understood. Theory is useless outside human application. If only a minority understand theory, only a minority can execute theory; thus theorists require a horde of executives who must control the human condition, control our interactions and our relationships. Because human beings have a tendency to resent such control, we need force to maintain the hierarchy of theorists and executives — police, army, the "enforcers of law."

Despite all academic criticism to the contrary, my book *I am Woman* is a theoretical text. It was arrived at through my meticulous ploughing of the fields of hundreds of books on the European colonial process — capitalist theory, de-colonization, law and philosophy — from the perspective of Indigenous law, philosophy, and culture. My understanding of the process of colonization and de-colonization of Native women is rooted in my theoretical perception of social reality, and it is tested in the crucible of human social practice. The stories and the poetry bring the reality home and allow the victims to de-victimize their consciousness. For Native women, and a good many white women, *I am Woman* is empowering and transformative.

I am Woman takes the lives of women very seriously. The book walks gently across the ruined cages, the glass of which I shatter on the very first page... "How can one reduce one's loved ones small...minus the colors and the music that moves them..." — to fields of blossoming flowers at the end. The book is filled with story, and it is guided by theory presented through story — the language of people. It is a spiraling in on the self who rose above all the myriad obstacles the colonial *and* patriarchal process presents for women. More. The book spirals out from the self, in a dogged and heartfelt way, to touch the heart of woman.

By talking to my readers as though they were truly there in my heart, both the point of victimization and the point of resistance become clear. The value of resistance is the reclaiming of the sacred and significant self. By using story and poetry I move from the empowerment of my self to the empowerment of every person who reads the book. It is personally dangerous for me to live among dis-empowered oppressed individuals. "When they come to get me, I want to know: who is going to be there with me? Because I am not going willingly." So said a young white woman speaking on the possibility of organized state violence against the women's movement in this country. I want to know who is going to be there with me, resisting victimization — peacefully or otherwise, but always stubbornly and doggedly struggling to reclaim and hang on to my sacred self.

Originally published as the first issue of *Gallerie: Women Artists' Monographs*, September 1990, now out of print.

Lee Maracle

Lee Maracle is a writer, a poet and a skilled orator who speaks around the world on subjects ranging from medicine to social conditions. Maracle brings to all her work a profound knowledge of contemporary society and her own history.

Maracle grew up in North Vancouver. Speaking of the forces that militated against her vocation in *I Am Woman* (Vancouver: Write-On Press, 1988), Maracle says, "I wanted to be a writer when I was still a 'wharf rat' from the mud flats.... I did not want the 'fame' that went with it. Part of being colonized is the need to remain invisible. They erase you, and you want to stay that way." Through years of Native Rights activism, working for money, raising her children, and struggling with ill health, Maracle worked at becoming a writer, eventually emerging in recent years as one of the strongest voices on the contemporary Canadian scene. She has developed a unique style, combining story, poetry, philosophy and social theory in both fiction and essays.

Maracle's other books include the autobiographical *Bobbi Lee: Indian Rebel* (1976, reissued Toronto: Women's Press, 1990). *Sojourner's Truth*, a collection of stories, was published by Press Gang Publishers in 1991.

Maracle's first novel, *SunDogs,* (Penticton: Theytus Books, 1992) takes readers on a cultural and spiritual journey into the heart of First Nations' country during the Oka crisis.

In a second novel, *Raven's Song,* (forthcoming, Vancouver: Press Gang, 1993), Maracle tells the story of Stacey, a young woman who grows up bridging two vastly different cultures. Raven pokes fun, imparts wisdom, and raises critical questions about Native and white relations.

GALLERIE PUBLICATIONS BOOKS BY WOMEN ARTISTS

WOMEN ARTISTS' MONOGRAPHS

Support the series with your subscription and SAVE: $16.95 for 4 issues

Forbidden Subjects: Self-Portraits by Lesbian Artists. Lesbian artists explore identity, community, subjectivity, self image, love and survival. $8.95

Come Spring: Journey of a Sansei by Haruko Okano. Japanese-Canadian sculptor and writer Okano remembers her childhood experience of trauma and displacement, looking at issues of racism and recovery. $6.95

Art and Survival: Creative Solutions to Environmental Problems by Patricia Johanson. Johanson works with scientists, citizens groups, engineers and urban planners to create her art as functioning infrastructure for modern cities. . . $5.95

Art and Healing by Jan Crawford. A young artist describes her fight with cancer. She explores the age-old healing tradition of art-as-therapy, discussing how art can heal and reveal our inner life. 13 colour plates. $5.95

In My Country. Nine Canadian artists consider the best and the worst of their country. Where do we see the seeds of the world we want?. $3.95

Meat by Sue and Mandy Coe. A shocking indictment of the Meat Industry; a discussion of the power of "witnessing" as a tool for change. $3.95

OTHER PUBLICATIONS BY WOMEN ARTISTS

Artists' News. The newsletter of Gallerie Publications' Women Artists' Registry. Women artists share news and resources, practical ideas and creative strategies. Subscriptions $8.00 per year. For free sample copy and information on the Registry send stamped, self-addressed envelope.

Women Artists: Contemporary Quilts. Issue 9 of *Gallerie: Women Artists* with a special focus on contemporary quilts. 14 quiltmakers discuss their work including performance artist Suzanne Lacy. $6.95

Surviving Childhood: Deciphering Sexual Identity; Healing the Wounds of Sexual Abuse. Issue 8 of *Gallerie: Women Artists.* Artists describe how their work can uncover and heal the wounds of sexual abuse. $6.95

1988 Annual: Women artists including Judy Chicago, Sue Coe, and Nancy Spero present their work. Articles by Bettina Aptheker and Judy Grahn. $12.00

1989 Annual: Lois Mailou Jones, Faith Ringgold, Tee Corinne, Muriel Castanis and many other artists present their work. Articles by Joan Borsa and Michelle Parkerson. $12.00